SEXUAL

PSYCHIC

SEDUCTION

Edited

by

Psi Research Institute

SEXUAL

PSYCHIC

SEDUCTION

ISBN: 0-9763862-2-4

Table of Contents

Introduction

What is sexual psychic seduction? It is about using the power of your mind to attract sexual relations to you. You create your own reality everyday with your mind. What you wear, where you live, everything that you currently are was created by the power of your mind.

What you will be able to do after reading this book is to increase your ability to attract sexual relations. To do this we have to change the way you direct your thoughts, your thinking. Once you are aware of your thoughts, you will be able to direct them to the goals that you desire.

Awareness is an empowering concept. There is much more around you in your everyday life then you are aware of. Your routine thinking has blinded you to the rich psychic environment that surrounds you.

Just because you can't see something doesn't mean it doesn't exist. Have you ever seen a radio signal, a television wave, a loud noise, the smell of a rose or a thought impulse from your mind. You may never have seen these things but you know they are real and do exist.

By opening your mind to the existence of things that you can't see, you have opened your mind to the reality of psychic phenomena. It's not as important to know how it works, but that it does work. You may not know exactly the mechanics of you cell phone but that doesn't prevent you from using it to make your life better.

This book will provide you with mental tools to increase your psychic ability, to surround yourself with the sexual relationships that you desire. Open your mind and let the universe provide for you what you want.

Sexual Psychic Seduction

Good Vibrations

As we discussed in the introduction of this book, there are things you can't see, that are real and that can be used to better your life.

If radio signals can be picked up by radios and television waves by TV sets then what would prevent your mind from sending out psychic vibrations at frequencies that another person could receive in their mind?

Invisible frequencies or "vibrations" are a normal part of our life. Focusing on the frequencies that another person can pick up on is our goal. We want to harness the power of your mind to control the content of the vibrations you send to another.

Is it unethical to try to secretly send people messages through your mind without them knowing it? The simple answer is no. Everyone sends out non-verbal communique that others pickup on in a subconscious way. What you will learn is how to control the message of those signals.

The psychic message that you will be sending is seduction. Seduction is defined as the alluring of another into a sexual relationship, whether that be for a night or longer.

Sexual seduction is not trickery or making someone do something they don't want to. Often times a direct verbal approach will fail because of the social conscious barricade that has been instilled in us from children.

Instead of breaking down the obstacles that prevent healthy sexual relations, sexual psychic seduction passes through them to the unconscious mind of another and lets that part of the person decide what they want.

Thought = Energy = Power

The circumstances of your life at this moment are the result of what you have attracted to you and let become a part of it. This is a foreign concept for many people. If this is true then negative things that have happened to you are the result of your own thinking.

You might not of been thinking of losing your job when you did, but the actions from your thinking allowed it to happen. If your awareness had been greater could you have prevented it from happening either through harder work or finding a different job to begin with?

Everything that becomes a reality started off as a thought. Although thought does not always produce instant results, it can in some instances. Most of the time though, thought works it way through various circumstances to create what your goal was.

As you take more control over your thoughts, your power to influence events around you will increase. You can then guide the way things happen as opposed to just waiting for it to come.

Everyone knows someone who is constantly complaining about their health and seem to always be sick. The thoughts of their own ill health feed upon themselves to continue the cycle of "I think I feel bad there for I do feel bad."

Although negative thoughts are a normal part of the human thought process, it's the reinforcement of these thoughts that materialize the very things you hope to avoid.

Because of the jumble of thoughts going through your mind every second, minute, hour, day and year of your life, most do not bring with them the power to reshape reality. The mind does listen though.

Your physical reality is referred to as the 3rd dimension. A photograph is an example of the 2nd dimension. The 4th dimension you live in while you dream. The higher the dimension the easier it is for your thoughts to take shape.

In the 3-dimensional world to fly you must physically enter a flying machine (airplane, hot air balloon, glider etc.). In the 4th dimension you simply think of flying and you are, no other constructs are needed.

The reason that your thoughts more readily take shape in higher dimensions is that your thoughts are close to the same frequency as the higher dimensions.

Learning strategies to tap the higher dimensions will have a quicker and more powerful effect than would ones that are rooted in the 3rd dimension.

One of the keys to using your thoughts to manipulate your life and your life's events is to see it within you. It's the concept of visualizing. When you see your goal in your mind as if it was actually happening, you are affecting your 4th dimensional awareness.

The mind's eye is where you construct the reality you wish to live in. When you are using your mind power to seduce others, clarity of thought is very important. What you see in your mind and the way you visualize it must be as clear as you can get it.

You need to reach out to other person, touching them

with your mind. You are using your mind for arousal of another person which is a form of telepathic communication. Telepathic communication can be broken down into 3 basic forms.

One way is called instinctual telepathy. This is the type that results when the energy of one etheric body hits the etheric body of another. The etheric body is the invisible aura that surrounds every human. There is even a special type of camera that can take a picture of this outer shell. When you get involved in a close relationship with someone and you both have the same thought, idea or say something at the same time, this is an example of instinctual telepathy. Instinctual telepathy picks up on another's thoughts naturally and without any direction being given by the mind.

A second form is called mental telepathy. Mental telepathy is the conscious direction of thought directed towards another person. You have a specific goal in which you want another's mind to perceive without interference from their conscious mind.

The third form of telepathy is called intuitional telepathy. This where you are receptive and able to communicate with higher things and purposes. This type of telepathy does not involve itself with physical manifestations at a base level such as sex and money. This type of mind power is not the goal of this book.

Two ways to limit your telepathic abilities are to become obsessive about your goal and to let fear of failure cloud your thoughts. When you are doing advanced sexual psychic seduction techniques you must have a calm, care-free mental attitude. Do not waste your mental energy by worrying or fearing that you will not obtain what you want.

The right attitude is that of confidence and assurance, you do what you need to do, and then go on. When you are trying to make a mental thought based connection with someone, you are creating a non-physical link between yourself and that person. When you carry negative emotions into that link, it creates energy that repulses the original thought work.

If you are worried about failure or not getting success, these powerful emotions act like a boomerang and return back to you because there is more of an energy link on your side and less on the other person's side.

When you are doing advanced psychic seduction you must have a non-obsessive "I don't care" attitude. Do your techniques but don't put a huge amount of energy into worrying about failure or success.

At first you will be a little unsure of yourself. Just relax, be confident and do the psychic techniques and when your done, move on to something else knowing that your techniques are taking effect and working without your further attention needed.

You can think about it from time to time but let the confidence of attitude carry the way. Reinforcement of your goal not fear of failure will guide you.

You will succeed if you have knowledge, use it correctly and then let the power of your mind go to work. This is important and once you see that you can get anybody you desire, you will have incredible confidence within yourself that goes into effect even before you start the techniques.

Detach your intense desire when using this type of mental power and you will find quicker results.

Sexual Psychic Seduction

The Human Transponder

When you begin to apply your psychic seduction techniques on the person you are trying to win, your thoughts are not just whims in the mist; they are concrete and real and are actually having an affect in the environment. When you understand about the frequencies of the mind, you'll see how other people's thought waves can easily get in sync with you. And your environment will assist this process.

Your brain is capable of producing a wide variety of frequencies. Focusing and tuning in on the frequency that will project your sexual desires to another person is what this book is geared towards.

A key to sexual psychic seduction is the brain frequency between the alpha and theta range. The alpha state ranges between 7-13 cycles per second (cps). The theta state ranges between 3.5 - 7 cps. The optimum SPS (sexual psychic seduction)state ranges between 6 - 8 cps.

There are 3 main reason why you need to change your brain wave cycle when you want to sexually arouse someone with your mind:

1) Your brain waves will become closer to the natural frequency of your environment. When you lower your brain wave cycle to a cycle that's closer to your environment, your mind will have easier access to change the environment.

2) When your brain waves are slower and your mind is more relaxed then your body will be more relaxed. Less blood

needs to be pumped to your body functions which allows more blood to pumped to your brain. Your brain is more nourished when you are relaxed.

3) You can become more focused when your brain waves are slower. Increasing your focus allows access to different parts and functions of your brain. Your awareness and your ability to use your mind will become easier and stronger. This will greatly effect all your SPS work.

Learning to use the brain frequency between the alpha and theta ranges is the first step to successful sexual psychic seduction. When your brain state is at this rate, you will be in a relaxed, daydream like state without being asleep.

When you are in this SPS state, your thoughts break from the barrier of time and space. You can send your thoughts around the globe and will have hardly any barriers in their way. This means that your thoughts will have the ability to get into the thoughts of someone else. You will be able to program the person in this state.

Tuning your mind into the SPS state is the key to mind manipulation and influence.

Dimensional Weaving

Understanding the concept of dimensions is very important for sexual psychic seduction. The first thing you should realize is that all dimensions are merged together.

When someone talks about moving up to another dimension, the moving up does not mean going up as in vertical up. Nor does it mean an upward change of awareness. Higher dimensions are up, below, around, inside, and every which way around and within you. They are all merged together like the ingredients in a mixing bowl. This means that you are within higher dimensions other than this 3rd dimensional world around you.

The word dimension is just a name given to the concept of reality levels. The 3rd dimension is a name given to describe your current world around you.

You cannot see or experience other dimensions that you are not tuned into. Like a television, if you are watching channel 6 then you are not tuned into channel 9.

Experiencing other dimensions works in exactly the same way that a television or radio works. You have to change the wavelength of what you are now to where you want to be. The difference between dimensional worlds is their wavelength.

What is the secret to tuning into different dimensions? Visualizing in the SPS state is the key! Visualizing is seeing something in your mind that you want to manifest in the world around you.

When you are in a higher dimension it is your thoughts or the images that you create in your mind that manifest around you instantly. This is why you can fly in your dreams or do just about anything else that you can think of.

The same part of your mind that takes care of all your bodily functions knows how to interact with the higher dimensions around you. If you see something in your mind's eye (your imagination) your higher self will go about and manifest it for you. Your mind will create your thoughts around you depending on what your hold in your mind's eye.

It is best to focus on one person at a time until you get the swing of things. Once you have practiced a bit, you can easily influence many different people. You can use your sexual psychic seduction ability for whatever sexual goals you have.

Whether you know the person very well, are an acquaintance, or they are a complete stranger, spend a few days planning what to do. A good strategy is a great advantage. Keep a list of where you've seen them the most, their most noticeable features, the clothes they wore that you enjoyed, how they talk, expressions that they use the most, how they hold themselves, how they speak and what their skin looks like. Make a journal of everything that is the essence of that person.

Be careful with this practice because you are definitely not trying to be a stalker. You don't want information on their every move. What you want is to make note of the most noticeable things so when you do your SPS power work you will have an easier time visualizing them. You want the stuff that strikes you and the stuff about their body (hair, speech, features, etc) only. If they are good with animals or like to watch TV, this is not important stuff to note.

When you start to use the specific visualizing techniques, you will want to see them as clearly as you can in your mind; as if they were in front of you. You might think that you can remember these noticeable features, but when you get down to the work, you will notice that your ability to visualize will be limited until you practice.

It might be hard for you to visualize the sound of their voice but it might be easy to you to visualize the way they do their hair. This is why it is good to have a whole bunch of characteristics ready.

As you practice, you will get better at visualizing the person. The reason that you note the place where you see them the most is that if your visualized image of them starts to fade and you can't seem to hold what they look like in your mind you can simply imagine the place where you see them the most and then recreate their image before you take them back to your inner world.

When you use visualization what you are doing is subconsciously implanting your desires into their thoughts. To effectively visualize, you must have a quiet place to do this. Your surroundings have to be quiet. It is best to begin to learn to visualize with the lights out. Eventually you can keep your eyes open (in public places) and your visualizing skill will be developed enough to do in the broad daylight.

To start out with your surroundings must be free of drafts, loud noises and other distractions. Nothing is more annoying when you are in a deep mind state and the telephone rings, or you hear the neighbors making noise. Obviously it's not possible to get rid of all the noises but do your best to close yourself away from most noise.

It is better to do the visualizing while you are sitting.

Often when you are lying down you get too relaxed and you fall asleep. Also, at first it is easier to visualize your inner reality when your head is in the same vertical position that it is throughout your daily life. That is why sitting is good.

Just sit down and perhaps lean against the bed or a wall or whatever. The point is to get in a comfortable position so you can concentrate on your mental seduction work instead of shifting frequently to get comfortable.

When you are ready move your visualizing into your own 'place' for sexual relations. This can be any place that you choose. It can be an exotic tropical setting or in the back room of your office. It can be where you see the person the most or an imaginary place of your own creation.

Take time to create this place in your mind until it feels like a place you are comfortable in and feel powerful in. You are in control in this place so make it just what you want. One thing is important though, do not let this place be where you are now. This is because you want to remove your self from what's around you as much as possible in your visualizing. Closing your eyes and imaging yourself in your own bedroom or living room tends to keep your brain in a 'waking' state more than in a removed state.

Your new 'place' created in your mind needs to be free from all negative vibrations. You should also have a different place for each person you are using SPS on.

You are now going to be visualizing the person that you've had you eye on; the person or persons you want to have a sexual relationship with. Put the person you want in this visualized surrounding that you have created. This gives your brain waves and their brain waves a chance to melt together so they will be ready for your influence.

The key to visualizing is to see something in your mind as if it is really happening. To see something in your mind as if it is actually happening just takes practice. When you visualize always put yourself in the picture as if you were seeing it through your own eyes, just like any situation you are in now. <u>Do not</u> see yourself from a distance like you were watching a movie of yourself or floating above the situation.

In your visualizing, you do not see your face unless you visualize looking into a mirror. You must be in your imagination as you are in your daily life. If you visualize yourself walking down the street, you won't be able to see your face, top of your head and back, you will be able to look down and see your legs, arms and chest just like your "real" life.

Practice makes perfect. You are going to want to spend at least three times a week for a minimum of 20 minutes each session visualizing your sexual goal.

Even when you have honed your skills to a high degree and can effectively visualize with your eyes open and in public you have to keep your expectations real. When you are in a crowded place and you use SPS techniques on a person, they might not drop everything and come running to you. They still might feel attracted to you but maybe they have to go, or maybe they are going the opposite way.

Because you didn't get immediate attention from them does not mean that you were unsuccessful, it's just the reality of the situation. There is a little more advantage if you are in a place where you have an opportunity to meet this stranger or if you know you might see them someplace again. These are opportunities.

Even just seeing a person once, if you know you will see them again, puts your SPS to full force. They will think about that first moment seeing you and then things will start to develop as they see you here and there again.

If you are practicing on a person that you know quite well, you will see results much quicker. You will have more opportunity to see the signs, more opportunity to influence them directly in front of them, and you will have more opportunity to let them come to you.

If your skill is very fine tuned, you can have most persons you frequently or casually interact with. Reach for this goal if you want. It takes time to get this good but it can happen with practice, determination, creativity and patience.

How it Works

It is important that you be in a particular brain state in order for sexual psychic seduction to be effective. You can get success with your mind in an ordinary waking state but your manipulation of the reality around you becomes more pronounced when you are able to lower your brain state.

When you are in the SPS state the effect will be the most pronounced upon the mind of the person you are wanting to influence. Your thoughts will be able to get to them more clearly with more power.

To give you an idea of the difference between doing SPS arousal work in your normal waking Beta state versus the SPS state... if you were visualizing your fingers touching someone in an erotic way while in the Beta state, the person would probably feel or sense nothing. If you were in a SPS state and you imagine the touch of your fingers on someone in an erotic fashion, the person would actually feel the touch as if your physical hand was actually touching them. That is how real it will fee for them.

Here is how your thought waves get into the mind of another person. Your thought waves arrive outside of the skull of the person you are using SPS techniques on. From the outside of their skull, this incoming wavefront sets up a resonance or a vibration in the sections of their cranial bone. Setting up a resonance of these sections occurs when the wave front bounces around equally to all the cranial sections.

If you made a cross section of the skull as this event occurred and if you could see the resonance being established, the wavefront vibrations would form a pentagram, touching all

5 sections of the cranium. Electrons are formed from this action and an electric pulse flows to the part of the brain that turns electrical impulse into thought.. thus thought is perceived by the person your are influencing. When the SPS techniques you are using are perceived by the person they are gentle, natural and very arousing. The person just experiences getting turned on in a natural way, as if it came from their own mind! Depending on the sex, they will start getting wet or hard and physically aroused in a natural way.

The most important aspect to your SPS work is the concept of touch. You must develop this feeling of touching more strongly that your ability to see while visualizing.

When the person is firmly in your visualized place, imagine that they are naked. Your next step is to reach your hand out and touch them. Use your visualized sense of touch to erotically caress them with your hand. If you loose the entire image of the person that is alright. Just concentrate on the area of their body that your are touching.

Using touch in your visualizing is the most important aspect arousal and seducing. This skill must be developed and you should practice touching things in your mind so you can feel it with your mind. You don't want to <u>see</u> your self touching as much as you want to actually <u>feel</u> the touch.

In your practice session, imagine touching things like a soft pillow, ice cubes, sharp objects, rough objects, anything that can help you fine tune your sense of touch within your mind.

When you touch someone in your visualizing you are creating a tremendously powerful link to that person. It is this "magic touch" that will drive them into a frenzy and eventually draw them to you. Explore them with your fingers, palms, hands and take your time. Let your imagination explore every sensation of touch on the person.

If your are touching their genital area then explore their pubic hair, wetness, hardness, tenderness, softness, warmness, hotness, quiverness, etc. Let your fingers and hands explore different areas of their body such as their nipples,ears, mouth, inner thighs, hair, knees, etc. You create in your mind what you are doing to them and what they are experiencing.

No other technique in your mental ability can compare to this use of touch and there is no way for the person to avoid it. If you do it for only about 5 minutes, you will create effects that may last several hours. The person will begin to feel warmth, tingling, hardness, wetness and turned on feelings.

The longer you use this magic touch the excitement that will build up in the person will be hard to resist and they will have a strong attraction towards you (even if they don't know who you are). They won't even be able to fight these feelings because they are coming from deep inside of them "on their own".

Remember this will take a little practice but it will hit them even on the first try no matter how slight. Also remember to really feel the touch even if you cannot see it.

In you inner eye, you can totally feel the sensation of touch as if you were really doing it. You will like to explore the person's body in so many ways.

Visualizing scenarios is the second part of this magic touch. It should come only after you have mentally touched the person. If you are mentally touching someone in their genital area, start to visualize the person's reaction. Look up at their face and see their reaction. Watch and make their body move and quiver under your touch. Begin to visualize them in the way that you want to see them reacting to your touch all the while still feeling the caressing as if it was happening.

By bringing in reactions, you are starting to create an entire scenario of passion and lust. Bring in to your newly developed sense of hearing and tasting and talking within your mind. Hear the person's moans along with your touch. Hear their voice. Begin to make things get passionate but try to do more of the giving than to visualize them doing the giving.

You want to focus on their arousal and stay away from a fantasy experience for your own pleasure. You might get aroused by this but try to stay in control and make sure do most all of the giving.

When you begin to add full visualizing to your mental touching, you can see the back that your are touching, you can see the breasts that you are stimulating, you can see the thighs that you're caressing. Make sure that the person becomes very aroused by this in your mind and especially make sure that they crave you and want you more and more!

Try to avoid getting too fast with all of this. The slower you do your visualizing scenario and your visualizing touching, the more erotic it will be for them. This creates a deep passion within the real person and it continually hones your concentration.

If you add to your visualizing some oral movements on the person, you also create stronger feelings within the real person. Remember that you are doing the stuff to them and they are getting horny by it in your mind. You're not trying to get off on this. If you do, your heart will start to beat faster and you'll start to come out of your SPS state. If you get turned on while doing these visualizations, then keep control and keep your eyes closed and channel this sexual energy into your visualizing.

Whatever you use your visualizing for, make the person react the way you want them to react and this will manifest in the real 3rd dimensional world. The powers of your mind can be so developed for what ever you want.

If you wanted someone to get turned on by you whenever they had a shower by themselves, then visualize this daily and sure enough they will be thinking of you when they shower. You create the reality and the relationship you want as it develops.

First the physical sensation hits them without any awareness. Then they become aware that they are getting a little turned on. And then thoughts of you come into their mind. These thoughts may be very obvious to them and they will consciously feel attracted to you or these thoughts will be a little more deeper and their unaware mind will make more of the connection.

It is better to establish a deep foundation within the person's psyche. They might get a little turned on but are not really thinking about anybody specifically. Their unaware mind has often had some links to certain people and then when they see those people in their daily life they become more aware of their attraction to them.

As this attraction increases, the times when they get aroused by the thoughts of a certain person will come into their conscious awareness. This is how it might happen in the person you are working on. They might not instantly think hot thoughts about you but their subconscious mind will be associating these arousal felling to you and then it will manifest as the person becomes more attracted to you.

So if you don't see any instant reactions, don't worry because their subconscious mind will be programming their conscious mind to be drawn to you. Their subconscious mind will seek you out only and will not think that these arousal feelings are coming from someone else.

Allow this to happen an you'll see that the person will come to you eventually. This won't take long. Remember, since this is a natural feeling that will be developing inside of them (as if it was under their own accord), you probably will go through the usual motions like dating, getting to know each other and all that sort of stuff. Don't worry, you will be continually imbedding deep passionate feelings within them and they will manifest quicker than if you went through the usual motions without using mind power techniques.

These feelings that you are visualizing upon them will last forever. They will not feel turned on until the end of time, but they will feel attracted to you in the same way you can be attracted to someone over decades. If you are doing these techniques while the person is sleeping then they will dream about you. Influencing while the person is asleep is more effective than if the person is awake. Both can be effective and both should be practiced.

When you decide you've had enough of your session, keep your eyes closed and return your mind to to your imaginary starting point. You can still see that the person is lying down or wondering why you stopped, but try to explore your "place" again before you open your eyes.

Waking Techniques

Now for the techniques that can be put to use when you are near the person or are talking to the person. You still need to do the same "magic touch" but you don't have to close your eyes to do it.

If you properly practice the touch sensations you don't need to visualize anything except the imaginary sensation of touch. Lets say the person is near you but they are not looking at you. Just experience the touch sensation in your mind like in the visualizing work explained in the previous chapter.

Your brain will still produce SPS waves because you are harnessing your imagination and it will be associated with your SPS visualizing when you are alone.

Just feel your hand go up their dress or down their pants in a gentle erotic manner. In your mind, do the same finger caresses and erotic touching that you would do if it was really happening.

As you are doing whatever you are doing physically (walking, sitting, etc.) keep your mental thought on your touching and caressing of that person but do an added techniques and remove their clothes in your mind and try to imagine them behaving in your mind like you want them to be (preferably becoming turned on by your touching and caressing).

At first, until you get good at live mental seduction, you can stick to just the touching sensation. In time it will be easier for you to visualize nakedness and eroticism while your eyes are open. The more your mind is mentally working on this the more SPS waves you will be producing and the more of an effect this will have.

You want to hone your skills so good that you can be in a public place with your eyes totally open yet can visualize something in such detail that you loose focus of the 3-dimensional world around you.

Don't forget the most important thing is the feeling of touch as if you were actually touching them. This is the most important thing even as your other skills become slowly developed. This is where your focus and concentration should go.

Your mind must remain relaxed and not in an intense will power type of concentration that is mind draining. Relax and enjoy the touch sensation plus the added confidence that will make your ability incredible without ever having to muster up any will power.

Doing Sexual Psychic Seduction techniques when you are near the person or doing seduction techniques when the person you want is not near you are two different skills that you have to develop.

There are advantages and disadvantages of both. If the person is near you, you will be able to see the effects. If the person is not in your presence, you won't be able to notice certain signs until you see them. Even though you will have less time to employ techniques if the person is in your sight, at least it will be easier to imagine touching them since that person is really near you. Get good at both areas of SPS and learn and develop both.

Learning both will enable your different skills to coverage and allow you to better picture them when you are not near them and you will be able to better visualize sexually when you are near them.

When you are touching someone sexually with your

mind, you will see many different things occurring. In the first stages of your training, the person being influenced will start to get turned on but might not consciously associate it with you. Eventually if you keep up the work on them, they will be drawn to you as their daily arousal keeps increasing. They will probably still hide it in public to an extent. If in a bar or in a relaxed place, they will probably flirt or unconsciously flirt.

If in public area like a work place, or school they will probably keep hiding it. Of course, it will get to them sooner or later and they will want to get to know you in whatever way they feel comfortable.

If you have been working on them for a couple of weeks and you know that they must be feeling some sort of deep attraction to you, they still might be a little shy to approach you (especially if they don't know you).

If this is the case, you should try and ease them through these new feelings by saying the first "hi", or aim to be near them alone for a a few minutes. This will create a chance for a meeting to take place which will increase the attraction because now the ice has broken.

When the person is within your sight, you will be able to see the effects of your mind control. It's very important for your development that you notice these signs. The signs show you just how you are progressing. The better you get the more of a reaction you get.

If you don't see a reaction at first, don't despair. It just takes a little practice and soon you will be seeing results. Once this occurs, you will become more and more motivated to do this work. As you mentally caress them (especially in the genital area) you will notice some of the following:

Touching in the area you are influencing, scratching in different areas, heat/wetness/erection produced, worried or puzzled expressions, shifting position, crossing/uncrossing their legs, touching their hair, arranging clothing, lighting up a cigarette, eating, laughing and any movement that seems to be a reaction or cover-up from your influence.

Sometimes the person will feel so turned on that they freeze up and try to leave the room due to the strong excitement factor. Sometimes the will feel drawn to look around and make eye contact (even if they are not consciously turning to look at you).

If you are doing this while speaking to the person on the phone, you might hear breathing changes, shifting noises, coughing, change in voice, changing topics and maybe even flirting. You, of course, will never let them in on your secret... NEVER. If you do, then their 'walls' might be too strong for you to break if you are inexperienced.

Take careful notice of their reactions and write them down for your study. If you are in a classroom or workplace, then you have a longer opportunity to do these techniques. Remember that the effect is taking place even if it is hard to notice. Have confidence in yourself and your abilities.

One of the best things you can do is to practice like crazy everywhere you can. And you can even practice on the same sex (even if you are not gay). If you are just practicing, then you are not trying to necessarily get someone turned on to you but rather you are trying to fine tune your skills and get reactions.

You can sometimes get a great reaction by doing mental touching techniques on anybody you see. If you practice everywhere you can, you increase your experience with different time lengths you have to work with.

In a public place, you can do these techniques without even looking directly at the person. Glancing is normal in social situations but staring may make the person uncomfortable. Check them out for a moment then look away and do your 'touches". Remember you want these techniques to be as secret as possible, so you never hold yourself like you are some god with incredible powers emanating from your eyes. When you get good, you can do other things while you are doing your techniques so you blend in completely with the people around you.

If you are behind the person at any distant, you can look at them but you should be smart when you have eye contact with them. Eventually you will be able to mentally touch them even while you are away from the person.

You will be able to carry on a conversation with them (not sexual in nature) at the same time your inner eye is feeling with touch whatever part of their body you want.

The less you do flirty type actions or conversations while you are doing mind power techniques, the more they will feel drawn to you on their own (since they think you are not provoking or trying to stimulate them with flirting.)

Keep the macho talk for the people who don't know these secrets. Make sure your conversations are fun, at ease and take an interest in them without any sign of direct flirting. This won't cause any blockages in the other person as your mind seduction powers hit their mind through the back door.

At first the person will become nicer to you and will become more talkative, more friendly. Rejection will also decrease after a couple of weeks if they have ever considered you "not their type". Their attitude is changing. Near the end, the person will probably feel drowsy a lot and be very affectionate towards you. If you are prone to doing long intense visualizing sessions, the person will have a brightness in their eyes and will also experience tiredness or insomnia.

Look for all these clues because they show you that things are changing. Just because you might not see a lot of noticeable reactions does not mean that you are ineffective with your methods. Every person is different and every person takes their own time. Just keep up with it and you will get that person sooner or later.

Besides physical reactions that you can notice, there will be a host of behavioral or overall reactions to watch for. These are signs of a person's changing attitude. These will begin from a few days after you start your work on them to when you finally get them (romantically, sexually or both). When this happens you should cease your mind power seduction and work on developing the relationship. If you keep doing it constantly, your mind will never learn that it was finally successful and thus can relax and enjoy the rewards.

Increasing the Force

As you begin to understand and use these techniques in your life, you can move beyond the basic methods and expand them to generate more power. Any books you can get on mind power or psychic techniques can be useful and you can grab bits and pieces from these different sources for your benefit.

The more you study things that are considered "occult" the more things you can find. Everybody finds their own ways of increasing their power to influence. Some practice Yoga, some do Tai-Chi, some implement Karate training, some do Pranayman (yogic breathing), some get into crystals, some use subliminal tapes and self hypnosis techniques, some try magick, some try Tantric Sexual Yoga, some use brain wave inducing devices and the list goes on.

You don't have to do a lot of other "holistic" training to use the SPS techniques discussed in this book. You can if you wish, and it will increase your power, but only get involved in things that you are interested in. Interest is a powerful mind motivator that increases energy in and of itself.

First let's start with how to approach the Theta level of brain wave activity for SPS usage. Full conscious Theta manipulation is a very advanced subject and is only accomplished by a handful of people. Once you learn to achieve this state, mere seduction will not interest you.

Your brain waves emit a Theta frequency at the moment just before sleep. To incorporate mental based seduction techniques with this theta brain state is very easy to do in practice. This should never become your choice of techniques since it is only an enhancer to your Alpha work (a good enhancer that is).

The procedure is to do your usual Alpha visualizing but instead of doing it during the day or in an evening session, you want to do it when you are in bed and ready for sleep. Make sure you are ready for sleep and you won't need to get up and set the alarm or whatever. It's very simple, just keep up your visualizing as long as possible as you drift into a sleep. As stated in earlier chapters, you won't be able to remember the exact moment that you fall asleep, but let your visualizing be the last thing in your thoughts.

Of course, you cannot force this action and expect to consciously notice something. Just do your visualizing and soon you'll be asleep. The moment you do fall asleep, your Theta brain waves will pass through those thoughts or visualizations and give them a great burst of energy.

What usually happens in most situations is that just a few minutes or so before you are about to fall asleep, you change body positions and stop what you are doing (thinking, listening to music, etc.). You usually don't remember when this happens so it's hard to stop this. However with practice and self-programming, you will remain visualizing until you reach the Theta state.

After that you will stop visualizing (because you are now asleep) but all you need is that quick moment of Theta state the person you are working on will actually feel your mental touches as if a hand was really there.

This will happen at that moment if your visualization remains stable up to this point. It will be quick and instantaneous, but it will have a great effect especially since you will be doing Alpha work (deep Alpha) as you slowly drift into sleep. It's like giving your visualizing a shot electricity at this moment of Theta.

It is important that you give some time to develop your own self by using your mind power skill. Spend equal time using mind power techniques to accomplish any goal and equal time using mind power techniques to develop self.

This way not only does your skill develop for mental persuasion but yourself as a person develops too. This will give you greater power in the long run. It's up to you what you want to develop within yourself other than mental abilities at seduction.

Spend some time visualizing other things to enhance your life (job, money, friends, knowledge, memory, etc.). Since you are in an Alpha state when you visualize, you will be in the perfect state to influence your own mind and hence your own reality with other aspects of important things.

Just visualize yourself as if you were all ready the way you want to be (e.g. with a promotion, with a new car, getting the audition, people treating you with respect, improved health, etc.).

One of the best things you can do that relates to mind power seduction is to spend time visualizing yourself with tremendous powers of of seduction. See yourself having easy success at it, see yourself influencing people easily, see other people being jealous of you because the opposite sex always falls for you, see yourself in the way that you want yourself to be after practicing mental seduction for a year, see yourself always with a grin knowing that you always get any person you want, or whatever.

This will quicken the results of your mind power seduction work because you are literally molding yourself into becoming powerful at it as you do become powerful at it.

Your diet can greatly affect your mental powers. Consuming a great amount of junk food and meat creates more work for your body; energy that could better be spent on mind development.

If you change your diet to that of less meat, less junk food and more fruits and vegetables, it won't be long before your visualizations become clearer and easier since your body is cleaning toxins and chemical additives out of your system. Your blood will be cleaner and this will nourish your brain and soul.

A healthy diet is very important since the body uses a lot of energy for digestion. The toxins in meat and chemically created foods take their toll even though you probably won't want to admit it.

Some of the chemicals are deliberately added to food for psychological manipulation (but that's a whole other story). Just try to eat healthy. And of course, exercise helps tremendously. You will gain more self-confidence, discipline and a healthy heart and mind.

Avoid drugs when doing SPS. You might think that it will enhance your work, but the 'enlightenment' you think you experience when you are high is chemically induced as opposed to the enlightenment you will experience from a developed, trained and practiced mind. This type of a high you won't loose, as your awareness grows and changes your life.

Often with drugs, you experience false awarenesses that go away as you come down or wake up the next morning. Combining drugs and mind power will ensure that your brain and mind never develop naturally and you will usually get caught in the 'trip' rather than focusing on the seduction.

Besides, if you ever learn to use your mind to literally take yourself into higher dimensions, your experience will be better than any drug!

Any mind power work that you do whether it's seducing people, travelling to other dimensions, out of body travelling to the past or whatever - you must have a little understanding of the Hermetic Philosophy*. This philosophy embodies the following principles:

1) Every human is a transmitter and receiver of impulses that exist and live within a specific wave length.

2) These impulses can be detected by a trained mind.

3) A human individual's subconscious mind is interconnected with the 'universal' subconscious. Within all individuals is the holographic duplicate of the entire universe.

4) Intuition is what you use to become receptive on this level.

5) The "feeling of knowing" transmits like a radio with this wavelength.

Now these 5 principles might not be too clear to you at first sight and this stuff can get very in depth (like any philosophy) ... so here is the basic gist that will apply to your mental powers.

To access the universal matrix (God, source of all consciousness), you are required to do things that seem 'counter opposite' to what you normally do.

•see appendix A

If you hope for things you are implying an uncertainty and a desire in the future which has yet to be fulfilled. If you imagine for things, you are visualizing the reality as if it already exists. There is a fine line between the idea of hoping compared to imagining (or creating). Here it is in even clearer terms.

Hermetic principles only operate in the present. If you want something in this material 3rd dimensional world, and it can be reasonably available to you, all you have to do is transmit that want to your subconscious mind.

Your subconscious mind will create your wishes only if the desire is transmitted properly to it from your conscious mind. Now here's that fine line...to make your desire successfully reach your subconscious mind (connected with the universe), your conscious mind must cease to exercise the desire. As long as the conscious mind wants something, the very act of wanting implies a future tense in regard to fulfillment.

Since you subconscious only deals with the present moment, any idea that is offered to it that is not in context with the present moment, that idea will be ignored. So the way that you apply this to your SPS work is that you must 'see' your desire as if it is already satisfied; as if you were doing it in the present.

This highlights our previous discourse that when you do your psychic touches you must feel it 100% and feel it as if it was happening in the present. The same goes for when you are doing seduction 'scenario' visualizing.

You must see and feel (with visualizing) the scenario as if it is happening in the present. Of course, you do this to the best of your ability and you will still get results even if you cannot feel the total present tense in your visualizing. The more you feel and experience your visualization work as if it were in the present moment, the quicker your results.

You can trick your subconscious mind if you can act or pretend. If you have a hard time feeling the 'presentness', you can pretend to feel it until it starts to feel real. If you hold yourself as if it is happening in the present moment (even though you are acting) you will find that real feeling of present awareness with your visualization will come to you easier.

Actors and actresses can do this very easily. They can feel a situation as if it were really happening in the present even though they are pretending to be someone else in someone else's situation. Once the performance is done though, they go back to their lives.

You can do the same but don't stop the feeling...continue it until your visualizing becomes real. And don't just feel (or pretend to feel) the present tense in your visualizing. When you are done, hold yourself or feel yourself as if you actually had touched or experienced something with that person.

If you had actually had a seduction encounter with someone for real, you would be thinking about it and remember it later wouldn't you? Do the same after your visualizing even if it is just a little bit. Keep the inner smile on your face because you got to caress and seduce the person that you desire.

You are training yourself to not only visualize the experience as if it was happening but you are training your self to live the experience as if it was a part of your life.

The Hermetic process is difficult for most beginners to apply. It requires you to believe that a desired condition exists before it can be manifested in the physical world. If you

WISH for a desired state, or HOPE that it will come to pass, you are automatically thinking in the FUTURE tense. As long as you want something, and the want remains unfulfilled (on this 3rd dimension), your aspirations are centered in the future and cannot be transmitted to the eternal now of the subconscious.

Hence, "desire nothing and there is nothing you shall not realize." Don't hope for your desire but live them and experience them as if they were happening. Do this with your visualizations and the way you carry yourself and feel your thoughts throughout the day. Your subconscious is a force that awaits activation and response through knowingness and certainty - thus "Blind Trust".

The mind is not capable of bringing anything to pass except when it is accomplished by the emotional counterpart of the idea. Feeling is the secret. You obtain your desire by feeling as if you already had what you want.

Resistance

Don't let the mention of resistance worry you. The SPS techniques explained in this book are not of a direct domination type. You are not forcing the feelings in the person you are trying to seduce. You are creating the feelings in the person and they will manifest in their own mind as if it was their own idea.

They will feel turned on by you or attracted to you with these techniques but they might resist it for many reasons. Perhaps they are married or live far away from you and they are avoiding thinking about you in these new ways.

Perhaps you were not normally their type and they are now confused as to why they find you attractive. Or perhaps they have a lot of peer pressure on what a lover should be or look like and showing up with you might make them "look bad" to their friends.

If this last one is the case, they are probably not mature enough to want to have a relationship with you anyway. Perhaps the person is normally very religious or has a very religious family...that person will probably suppress that they want to make love to you or avoid you because you come from a different religious background.

A lot of things might cause resistance and the person you are working on will try to suppress these new thoughts of desire for you. If they are resisting, they may show fear, withdrawal or begin to reject you.

Signs of resistance are things that you should notice and write down as with all noticeable reactions. By noticing reactions (good or bad) you will get a better idea of how to best approach your specific SPS techniques. Any noticeable sign should be considered proof that you are having an effect.

Signs of resistance show you that things are starting to work. All it means is that it will take longer for the programming to work. It does not mean that your efforts will not work. So here's how to deal with resistance completely which will further guarantee your success.

1) You can apply more intense and longer visualizing until the person's resistance breaks down. This will boost your power even if the person is suppressing their feelings or ignoring you. They will learn that resisting you will cause more visualizing on your part (of course, this is all on an unconscious level since they don't consciously know that you are using SPS techniques on them).

2) You can make a u-turn and visualize them very much wanting to achieve your goal yet at the same time in your visualizing, you give them the cold shoulder. While you visualize, make them want you and be so eager to please you yet you blow them off and reject them. This can also break the person's resistance completely because their mind cannot understand this influence or how to solve it and therefore the person is without defense.

3) You should cease doing your mind power techniques for a few days and then start again with more force. Continue this stop and starting if the person still resists. These pauses can be very effective because when you are holding off on your techniques for a few days, the unaware mind of the person feels that the pressure is off and the person begins to let down their defenses. When the defenses go down, all your visualizing begins to creep into the person's mind. When your mental images are blocked, they don't fade away. They just 'hang around' until an opening is made into the person's mind.

If the person is resisting, the visualizing you have done just waits and accumulates until there is a clear opening into the mind (such as when their defenses are down).

4) If the person is showing signs of being fearful about the new horny feelings you are creating in them, use your visualizing to slow down the passion. A gentle touch is often needed and then you can slowly build up the visualizing to erotic, intense levels. Visualize being friends at first and doing friend things (non-threatening) and then work up to lustful things after a few weeks. This techniques is important if you are trying to get a person to fall in love with you. You first visualize them being happy and comfortable with you; maybe laughing and playing and then put in the sexual scenarios when you have fully instilled the 'safe' scenarios.

5) If their unconscious mind can't handle the load of your influence, the person may even try getting away from you. This can occur even if they don't know you but they are resisting unconsciously. It doesn't matter how far the distance (the farther the better) since their defenses will go down and you can continue to do your work and your influence will gain entry into their mind much easier. The only problem is that you won't be able to monitor their reactions or signs of changed behavior, but that's okay because sparks should fly the next time they see you. And if you keep up with it during their move, they will begin to miss you like crazy.

If the person you are working on is resisting to some extent, then work with one or all of these techniques. Be very alert of their signs so you can use the best technique.

Some people get ill from energy/strength loss when trying to wrestle against your influence. Sooner or later, their subconscious mind will give up if you keep up the work. they will become yours. Every person is different and every situation is different so enjoy this diversity because it will fine tune your mental abilities and give you great experience at this type of work for future efforts.

The next two chapters will give you some ideas on some more ways to increase your power. One is radionics and the other is neurological triggers and anchors.

Hidden Technologies

There are many technologies that are kept hidden from the average person. The reason for this is that the potential that can be acquired with these technologies is unlimited...absolutely unlimited!

This reference to "technologies" is not to massive electronics, hardware, computers or billion dollar machines. The technologies this chapters refers to are mind-based, etheric connecting representations and connectors. This probably doesn't make much sense at this point but it soon will. In order to understand these technologies, you will need a refresher on the basics of our world reality.

The world around you and all the things in it are more than what you see. Your physical eyes can only see things which you consider physical because of limitations imposed upon all humans eons ago. That means that if you removed your limitations on what you eyes can see, then you will see many other things other than your physical surroundings.

Most people would think "Well what else is there to see?" The answer, LOTS! The things you see around you (including people and especially people) are not just physical in nature. They all have physical qualities but they also have other qualities as well. They exist on other levels.

One level of existence is on this physical world or more properly termed with the limitations of physical language... the third dimensional level. There are more levels than this third dimension, too many, in fact to count. One thing about these levels is that they all coincide or merge together like all the ingredients to make a pie merge together to form the completed pie.

With regards to radionics and other side technologies of the same family, the other level we are interested in is what is commonly call the "etheric" level. In actuality it is not called this, but this is an English word associated with this level and so it has stuck. Another level that you might of heard of has been called the "astral" level.

There are twelve overtones between levels (or dimensions or octaves). As stated before, the physical world is on the third dimensional level. The astral level exists on the first and second overtones of the 4th dimension. This "astral plane" is where you first go to when you leave your physical body. The "etheric plane" is lower than this astral level being more near and connected with the 3rd dimension.

Everything you *see* around you occupies higher levels other than this physical plane. To get to the point, all physical objects and structures (including people) have an etheric structure. Your physical body is not the only thing moving and functioning. You also have an etheric body; an invisible body that can be seen when you move up to higher levels or train yourself to see this level with your physical eyes.

All objects have an etheric body as well as a physical body. Cars, tree, books, food and even things that you can't see with your eyes such as music, vibrations, smells and thoughts!

Thoughts exist on higher levels such as the "etheric" or "astral" and can actually be seen when you access these levels. With skill, practice and knowledge your thoughts can be seen on this physical world so you can make an image of something appear in front of people if you had the know how. This might sound bizarre, but you and everyone around you actually do this already in a slightly different way.

Every human-made thing you see around you once began as a thought. Take a t-shirt for example. The design for the t-shirt began in someone's thoughts. The chemistry of the inks or fiber structure in the shirt once began and was created by someone thinking about it; using their thoughts to design it.

The machines that made the shirt first had to be thought of by someone (probably an engineer) who transferred their thoughts onto paper or computer as a new design. When you look at this concept of making your thoughts appear in front of people in this sense, it won't seem so far fetched and this is the first step for breaking down the limitations in your mind that you cannot "manifest things out of the blue".

The music a musician creates first begins in their thoughts. Whether it's the thought of how they want it to sound exactly or the thought of maybe "I should try this to see how this sounds". Once the CD is pressed, you have a physical object that once began as a thought: from the music, to the artistic design on the CD, to the actual machinery to make the CD...all components from thoughts.

This etheric level can be accessed in many ways from this physical level. One way to do this is through radionics. Radionics makes the connection or the link from the etheric plane to the physical plane and visa versa. A radionic machine can make a connection to the etheric body of a tree or to the thoughts (etheric level) of a person. And since you and your mind exist on all these levels at once, the radionic machine is really only helping your mind and awareness to make the connection. It is really your mind that is doing the work but with the help of the radionic machine to make the connection between the non-physical world and the physical world.

Compare it to reading a map. Your mind is really doing the work but it gets its bearings with the help of the map. the map is only helping your mind to sort and arrange information in the correct way to get your bearings and give you direction. The same applies with the radionic machine. It is only helping your mind to sort and arrange information in the correct way to get your goal working in the right direction and the best way.

Since radionic machines are only mind/etheric connecting tools, they do not have to be full of complicated physical components. That is why this knowledge is kept hidden from people.

Radionics works with settings that make links between thought waves to events and goals. Your mental link is a part of the machine often called the "well". This allows the flow of Prana, Chi, life force from the radionic device to reach your target or goal.

The setting (rate) that you establish with the "stick pad" increase the energy towards a specific action (your goal). The rate is a representation of a specific action that you wish to carry out. When you use radionic applications for the betterment of humans and the planet (such as finding missing children, preventing earthquakes, making soil fertile in dry Third World countries) then the full truth of radionics comes to you in time as a reward from the higher sources.

The highest form of radionics require the use of no physical instruments or things at all (internal radionics). It is just done by thoughts alone!

Since your thoughts are real on a higher level and not just some invisible wisp in your brain... you can create radionic machines that exist, run and are powered from a higher level all completely invisible from this physical world!

There are many advantages to this; some being that you are not limited to size, they are invisible to practically everyone on this planet and they can be extremely complicated without having to fork out any money to make them. And since all levels are existing together, someone in the physical world could pass through a component of an etheric radionic machine and never see or feel a thing.

If someone pulled you out of your body to the etheric plane or taught you how to access this plane on your own, you would be absolutely stunned at the massive, complicated, huge radionic setup that hovers above, blends with, and goes deep beneath our world.

The secret knowledge of "Psionics" is used to help with radionics. Psionics have many different descriptions. For the scope of this book, psionics is a way to amplify and trap energy by using conducive patterns.

A simple circle can be considered psionic in nature because the circle emits certain vibrations. A collection of circles creates even more energy and more power. All sorts of designs can do this if you know of which designs are inherently psionic.

The advantage of psionics is that you can use these energies for your own goals. Circular patterns generate a lot of energy and you can "charge" your goals in their center.

Since radionics are tools and machines for your mind/etheric functioning, the possibilities of uses are unlimited to what you can imagine. A list could be endless in radionic applications but here is a list of just some of the things you can do with a radionic machine. After you read this you'll see why radionics is so secret.

Radionic Uses

- Healing yourself or others of illness, disease, etc.

- Removing pests from your home without chemicals.

-Removing pests from crops without chemicals.

- Teleportation (moving your body around the globe with your thoughts alone)

- Levitation (raising physical objects into the air e.g. pyramid stones)

- Assisting with creative artistic endeavors.

-Personal protection.

_Psychic warfare if you are under attack.

-Removal of alien implants in you body.

- Accessing other dimensions and realities.

- Gaining secret knowledge.

- Reading the mind of others.

-Remote viewing (invisible cameras inside places of your choice).

- Telepathic communication between individuals.

-Wireless, invisible telephonic transmission.

- Military applications.

- Broadcasting music or images.

- Remote viewing.

-Programming water to have particular qualities to enhance personal development.

- Invoking the Light.

- Spreading love more creatively to anyone or anything.

- Winning the lottery.

- Dematerialization of physical structures.

- Breaking down time/space grids around your house for truly multidimensional living.

- Accessing higher levels of consciousness and help from higher sources.

- Inducing brain states and altered states.

- Programming specific energy patterns into anything.

- Transferring the energy of ancient power sources into psionic, radionic devices.

The list could go on and on. As you see, the question of morals comes up with many applications that are within your reach with radionics. You will find that any knowledge that comes to you on a higher level has to go through your conscious morals.

Most people think that because it is "higher knowledge" and awareness, it is always on the positive side. This is not so. Higher knowledge ca be used for both good and bad depending upon your choice. You can go to higher levels of awarenesses and dimensions and be a totally evil person. The control structures on this planet have been set up and implemented by negative beings that reside on higher dimensions.

A rule to follow is to keep your radionic work centered around love always, with no exceptions. For example, use your radionic machine for remote viewing to find missing children but don't use it to watch your favorite actor/actress take a shower.

Radionics is a branch of psionics which uses instruments to analyze and transmit information about and to etheric fields. The main key in radionic work is what is know as the "rate". The rate is nothing more than a language for translating psychic (mental) impressions into numbers.

Everything in existence can be converted into numerical form. This is very complex to get into so we'll keep it simple. Think back to your high school mathematics about the mathematical symbol called "pi". If you remember, this pi notation starts with 3.1416....and continues to infinity, it never ends.

What you math teacher didn't mention is that everything in existence is contained numerically withing the decimal places of "pi". If you were to convert your name into numbers, it would be found somewhere in pi. If you were to convert your bodily cellular structure into numerical notations, it would be found somewhere in pi. Your car's license plate could be found in pie. The time and date of you physical death is within pi. The memory and experience of a childhood trauma is within the pi notation. Feelings, thoughts, emotions, memories, goals, dreams, purposes, whatever, can be converted into numerical form and found somewhere in pi. The amount of atoms you will breath for the rest of your life can be found in pi. A radionic visualization can be converted into numbers and be found somewhere in pi. You name it, it is somewhere in pi. That is why pi is such a sacred mathematical notation and the pyramids are all built from this notational formula.

When you take a "rate" in radionics what you are really doing is accessing this pi notation (and other things) on a higher level; your mind is converting your thoughts or etheric structures into a numerical form. You don't need a calculator to do this. Your mind does it all since you are connected to all things on an unconscious level.

There are many different types of rates depending upon your radionic use. If you were to take a "contact" rate of a person for healing purposes, then this rate or series of numbers places you in contact with the person's etheric body. If you were to take a contact rate for a population of people, then this rate, or series of numbers, places you in contact with all the people's etheric bodies.

If you were to take a contact rate for a television satellite in orbit around the earth, then this rate or series of numbers places you in contact with the satellites etheric body. The contact will be maintained until you break it, something like an open phone line. Contact rates change each time you wish to get in touch with the structure, so there is no point in recording them for future use. If you are trying to make a connection with something, then you would take a contact rate. A rate is done with the dials on the radionic machine.

"Analysis" rates are used when you want to analyze something or to take a rate for something that will not change. This rate never changes and can be recorded and used for future use.

Other types of rates are pattern rates, broadcast rates, balance rates, light rates, organic rates, telepathic rates, just to name a few out of hundreds. Remember this field is very advanced and powerful.

The more rates you take with your radionic use, the more intricate of a connection you will make to the etheric energy and more success you will get with your radionic machine. Eventually, when you get very skilled at internal radionics, rates can be taken in the thousands just by your thoughts alone and connections will be made without you having to deal with any numbers. How could you possible do something like this automatically? It's simple...make a radionic machine that will do it for you and tap into it whenever you need to deal with massive amounts of rates (being creative)!

A rate can be taken with your radionic machine very simply; almost too simply to believe that it works. It's done with the use of what is known as a "stick pad". A pendulum can also be used after some preliminary practice but the stick pad is just as good.

This pad can be made from anything flat and smooth. Even though plastic and rubber are not natural, they work extremely well and that's why the top of a coffee can is sufficient. Copper and gold are the best.

The procedure is to pass or rub or stroke your right thumb on the flat surface with just enough pressure to move smoothly but with some friction. When you make the numerical connection your thumb will seem to stick or stop on the pad. A "stick" is hard to describe but you will know it when you feel it; it's different for each individual. Essentially the pad seems to "grab" the thumb and stop it. This is the connection.

What is really happening is that you are consciously asking your subconscious mind to access the pi notation by giving a sample number to try. As you stroke the pad, your subconscious mind is determining if the number that you have asked to access is the correct number to use. It if is not the correct number, your thumb will continue to pass over the pad as you stroke it. If it is the correct number, your subconscious mind responds by releasing minute amounts of etheric energy from you thumb to "grab" the etheric particles of the pad.

You don't have to worry about the technicalities of this procedure. Your mind takes care of it all. Just the action of you rubbing the pad slowly and asking your mind if it is the correct number, and knowing that your thumb will stick if it is the correct number, is all you have to do. Your subconscious mind takes care of the rest.

You know that when you eat something, the food will get digested in your stomach and pass into your body but you don't have to think about all the chemical, biological, neurological, physiological responses and mechanisms within your body to make this happen. You just eat and your subconscious mind takes care of the details.

If your conscious mind says that is how you will take a rate for the numbers and what will happen if the correct number is found, then leave it up to your subconscious mind to make it happen. Just rub the pad and your thumb will stick for you at the correct moment.

Radionics was one type of technology that was used in ancient civilizations, except they were far more advanced than ours. The mind/machines were much different than current radionic machines. Most were powered by natural earth grid energies and earth source energies found in crystals, stones, etc. They were also powered by thought, sacred geometry, sounds and more. Radionics have changed form and use throughout the ages. Medieval times revealed different types as well as some native aboriginal rituals (dancing, art, chanting, etc.) were radionic in nature (much different than modern radionics).

Radionics is like languages, there are so many different types, variations, branches, levels and uses. Some people can move stone with just their voices. They have a great knowledge of sound and harmonics and use the Earth as a type of radionic machine and dance a certain way which is their "rate". Their beats and steps upon the ground give them the "numbers" to make the connection between their mind, voices and their intent.

Their movement upon the ground reflects sacred geometry enabling them to generate even more power. This stuff can get very heavy duty and that is why it is rarely known and why you probably won't even believe in it.

If all this seems pretty far fetched, that' okay. This is nature's way of ensuring only certain people get this knowledge. But despite the rarity of this knowledge, you will be surprised at just how many people are involved in radionic research.

Some research is investigating the broadcast of sounds, tones, harmonics and frequencies worldwide without using any electronics. This might seem strange but wouldn't it be neat if your city was engulfed with music? Music that seemed to come from nowhere...music that penetrated all physical structure..music that healed and got rid of disease, fear and lower awareness levels.

Imagine being awakened in the middle of the night to amazing music that filled the skies and then days later the people in your city began physical and mental healing processes. Imagine 3rd world countries being engulfed with music and then days later, the Earth would begin to give food and growth in vegetation.

Imagine images being "broadcast" into television sets all over the country that interrupted all channels and revealed the truth about things (via radionic live cameras into the past). Wacko stuff eh? When the timing is right and the balance is centered..it will happen and it will start to bring people into new awareness and a new world in a positive way as opposed to the negative fearful ways (doomsday, Armageddon, aliens coming to get you, etc.)

When your mind is raised to new levels, your thoughts and use of your thoughts gain more power. You could use radionics for Sexual Psychic Seduction but once you see the unlimited power there is in radionics, seduction is just a lower instinct to be used and then graduated from.

Sexual Psychic Seduction

Sacred Geometry

So what's the deal with sacred geometry? Sacred geometry is the language of everything. You probably remember learning about geometry in school. "Sacred geometry" is a little different than the stuff they teach you in school.

The prominent aspect of sacred geometry is that everything (EVERYTHING) is a by-product of geometry and everything is connected by geometry. Geometry can be described mathematically and in all things there is a mathematical equation. Geometry can be found in everything in the universe and understanding of sacred geometry can give you the knowledge of all the universe.

When you understand the geometry in everything, you can begin to understand how life works and how we all fit together in the cosmos. Everything is created in a certain geometric way and has geometric properties..from DNA sequencing, to bodily cells, to trees, to dimensions, to language, to viruses, to music, to computers, to chemicals, to atoms. All of these are the basic geometric shapes. They are often called the Platonic Solids.

These are the components of so many things in the universe, from the energy fields around the planet to the energy fields around your body. They can even describe your cellular structure and your DNA if you know how to put them together. They even show exactly how the universe was created if you know how to understand them.

The most important image of sacred geometry is the Flower of Life because within it contains all of creation. Everything is created using this geometric pattern; everything from music, to language, to nature. This will not be readily seen to you if you have never seen or studied sacred geometry. Remember that sacred geometry is not just nice images on paper. These are motions and formations in multiple dimensions.

For example, the Flower of Life is made up of a collection of spheres that are interlocked. When they move in a certain way they can change form and create what is called a Tube Torus. this the shape of our universe (in 3D of course, depicted in a 2D way on paper).

One of the things that is most interesting is that all alphabets of all languages can be found in this image. It's all a matter of how you view it and what you view. If you picked a certain section of this tube and rotated it around you could clearly see each letter of the English alphabet or even the Hebrew alphabet.

When you convert the Bible in it's original Hebrew text into this image, the Bible can literally take shape in sacred geometry. This Tube Torus also show the gravitational force of the magnetic components of this planet. Even the ancient sites are laid out on one of the line spirals (called the Fibonacci spiral). This is a mathematical spiral that comes from a certain relationship of numbers depicting organic growth.

If you study the layout and placement of the ancient temples and structures, they all lay on this Fibonacci spiral and stem from one particular point in Egypt. The Fibonacci spiral can be seen all throughout nature (rams horn, nautilus shell, sunflower double spiral) and is the connection between music and the world around us. These 'symbols' occur everywhere in the universe. You cannot understand why all this has been hidden from you because full knowledge of this can make you a very powerful and enlightened human.

The Earth has energy fields surrounding it called grids. There are many different types of grids around the planet and they have many different geometric shapes. Ancient people knew about these grid lines or key lines as sometimes called. This is a free source of natural power if you can tap into the grids.

Nikola Tesla (the inventor of the radio) knew all about this stuff and designed some amazing things (most of which you will never read about). One of his biggest accomplishments that wasn't hidden from the public was his ability to broadcast electricity anywhere on the planet. With 8 special generators (Tesla Coils) placed in certain positions on the planet...he could tap into these grid energies and the result would be complete electrical power for the entire world.

It's interesting that these 'towers' would have to be placed at certain grid points coinciding with sacred geometric energy points. He knew something big but little became of this invention. Nikola did leave a big impression on the world though. Every time you plug something into your 60Hz outlet in the wall, you are using his invention (AC current).

A little bit of Tesla is everywhere...in every home and every business. He was able to see every invention in his mind perfectly even before he put it on paper. That's why he got it right the very first time when manufacturing a prototype. He was a genius at visualization, and he applied this for the good of all with his inventions. However the best of his work has been carefully hidden from the public.

So just how important is this information? Well sacred geometry can give you extraordinary abilities and can even give you the vehicle for moving into other dimensions!

Around your body is an energy field that consists of

two interlocking tetrahedrons. This image on a flat scale is also know as the Star of David (however the true knowledge of this image is still pretty much secret). On a full 3 dimensional scale, this image is a field of energy in the shape of two interlocking tetrahedrons called a Merkaba or Merkabah. You have this field around you however it's probably not activated.

You can activate it though with very hidden techniques. This energy field is your own 'vehicle' for moving into higher dimensions. Without giving away the secret, what you do is you get this field spinning around you at a certain ratio (Fibonacci ratio). When it hits a certain speed (0.9 speed of light), it bulges out like a disk and thus becomes your own consciousness driven vehicle for inter-dimensional travel.

UFOs are the same thing except they are created with electronic (external Merkaba). The one described above is an "internal Merkaba" and does not use electronics but rather certain breathing techniques, certain visualization techniques and a Love for all life everywhere.

When you get this field spinning, it bulges out to 55 feet. This Merkabah field is connected to your energy/chakra points. If you look at any yogic or eastern chakra chart, you will see the geometry of the double tetrahedron located at the 'Heart' Chakra.

Neurological Triggers

These techniques go back hundreds of years and can give you very sharp and clear inner visions. All types of information is stored in your brain and these techniques will bring this information instantly into your mind.

Give them plenty of practice and you will see. the pictures in your mind have to be very clear and powerful in order for your SPS power to be effective. The clearer the picture, the easier it will be for you to feel as if you are actually experiencing your visualized goal.

This first method will enhance your general clarity of your inner eye. Go outside during the day when the sun is shining brightly. With your eyes closed, look towards the sun. Ever heard of full spectrum lights? You can use these if you don't live in a sunny place. Look towards the sun for 15-30 seconds.

With your eyes still closed and looking towards the sun, massage your eyes for the same amount of time (15-30 seconds). This will produce lots of colors within your sight. Try to keep the colors in your mind and awareness as the colors appear. As you hold these colors in your mind and you can "see" them with your eyes closed, move your head away and back towards the sun a few times. do this movement for about 30 seconds.

Pause for a little and repeat the entire procedure a few times. Be careful no to rub your eyes to much; just a gentle massage. If you can hold the colors in your mind for more than 30 seconds, then continue to do so. The key is not to try and see the colors for a long time. The key is clarity in retaining what colors you see and the movement to and away from the sun.

What you are doing is stimulating the cones of your eyes which effect the direct intake of information going to your brain - thus giving you a more clear visualization ability.

The methods listed below may seem very basic but you should not underestimate the power they have. You just need to work with them to see for yourself.

1) This is an exercise for the lens of your eyes which will keep them flexible and will in turn enhance your powers of visualization. Start by looking at a book placed at a distance of 6 inches away form you and then look and focus on something far away (about 6 feet). If you wear glasses, don't use them for these exercises. Keep this focusing up back and forth without straining. This will give you great strength in the lens of your eyes which will make it better to visualize. Remember, when you visualize you are still using your eyes (just in a different way) combined with your imagination.

2) Place something that you can read on a wall at the same height as your eyes. This can be a page of newspaper or magazine or whatever. Stand as close as you need to in order to read the text. Next step back a little and try to read the text. Practice this everyday going just a tad farther back each time. You only need to practice about 1 minute a day and remember with all these exercises...Do not strain your eyes. You must remain relaxed.

In this next exercise you place a book as close to your face as is possible for you to still be able to read it. Read for a few seconds and then bring the book closer. Practice daily for about 1 minute.

The eye positions given now will open up hidden information in your brain as well as strengthen your memory, focus and learning capacity. These are natural neurological triggers that stimulate certain parts of your brains electrical impulses which creates specific results.

1) To recall visual memories, look straight ahead and then up to the left. Hold your eyes here for 25 seconds.This process forces your mind to recall visual memories when you are wanting to remember them. It will also strengthen your visual memory (visualization).

2) To access hearing or sound memory you need to look down and to the left. You must do this when you are visualizing something that has sound. Look down and to the left in your visualizing and your inner hearing will be more developed. This can be important because adding sound to your visualizing can increase your influence. If you are in that Alpha place of yours, maybe visualize a CD player at the bottom left corner of your sight. Look to that location in your visualizing and turn on the CD. Listening to music while you do Alpha work can bring total clarity in your visualizing over time.

3) To recall or enhance your touch memory or touch visualizing, practice looking down to the right. Practice these triggers in your daily life while you remember the appropriate memory (touch). When you visualize do these triggers in your mind's eye and enhance the appropriate sensation.

4) Looking up to the right is a very important trigger. While visualizing, this trigger can access new visual formations. For example, when you have created your imaginary Alpha room for seduction, lock it into this trigger by looking up to the right and telling yourself that your brain has now made a trigger connection with your Alpha place.

Over time, it will become easier to access this Alpha scenario when you start to visualize and look up to the right to bring this place into your imagination. Practice in the day for 1 minute looking up to the right and create new visual images.

5) Taste and smell can be accessed by looking straight down.

6) To access new sound forms, look straight and to the right. If you practice this and use it in your visualizing, you will open yourself up to all sorts of new sounds.

7) To recall auditory memory, look straight and to the left.

The key in this ..after you practice these exercises and recall the appropriate trigger (taste, touch,etc.), is to do all the movements in the order shown for about 20 seconds each. This will open up your "third eye" and it will make your visualization penetrate the deep depths of your mind (the subconscious).

This whole procedure can take only 5 minutes but will greatly enhance your visualization skill and creativity. These brain triggers might seem like a mystery to you. They have also been called anchors or links. They are just physical movements or stimulus that creates a link to a specific psychological process, feeling or experience.

Have you ever listened to a song you haven't heard in years and when you listen to the song you can remember the time in your life when that song was prominent? You might not remember a specific moment but the song might be linked with a "great summer" or an old lover. Even listening to a song years later still brings up the old memories or feelings you felt then. This is just a trigger that has been made between the physical hearing of song to a particular time in your past.

If you've never experienced this, then you are probably not old enough yet. The most prominent triggers of this sort are linked to you high school years since this is the flowering of emotional awareness combined with listening to a lot of music. (as most youth do).

The point is that music can create a great trigger within people but music is not the only trigger. If you have a had a bad experience while in a high place you will associate those negative feelings with a high elevation and thus - fear of heights. The same sort of trigger has been created with all sorts of things in people's lives whether fearing the boogie man under the bed to a dislike of a particular food that gave you a bad experience. Sexual triggers are also very powerful and the most common triggers occur when looking at a photograph and you remember or feel a past event.

You can use triggers to your advantage by creating your own neurological links with certain experiences or feelings. If every time when you felt very confident and incredibly happy you gently squeezed one of your ear lobes, you would be creating a trigger. The effect won't happen right away but if you keep up with the trigger for a few weeks or months, all you have to do is to do the exact same squeeze and the same confident feelings will come up.

When you are in the height of your visualizing seduction scenario, maybe touch a certain two fingers together at this moment. If you keep this up each time, when you are around the person you can do this trigger that you have created and your mind will emit all those vibrations and feelings that you were experiencing at the moment you programmed them into your trigger.

Even your basic Alpha state can be triggered to a discrete connection you make with your fingers, hands, ear lobes, or whatever. If you apply the exact same trigger every time you are in an alpha state, then it won't be long when you can induce these Alpha waves just by applying the trigger.

This is great if you are in public places and you wish to induce Alpha brainwaves when you are active. You can also create triggers with physical objects. You just link them with your experience over and over and soon you can just apply the trigger to get into that experience.

Triggers are only limited to your creativity. Here's one creative trigger. While you are visualizing your psychic touching, visualize yourself reaching up to the shoulder of the person you are working on. Place your hand on their shoulder gently for a quick second and then go back to your sexual visualizing.

If you repeat this for a few weeks in your visualizing, wait till the person is in front of you and then quickly place your real hand in the exact same quick way on their shoulder (as you did in your visualizing). You will be activating a double trigger here... your mental seduction Alpha influence and the person will quickly become turned on because you have induced this trigger to be associated with an erotic experience.

You can touch their shoulder quickly in an non-intruding way if it's a quick 'reassurance' type of touch or if you want to pull up your sock or something and you need someone to lean on for a second. It's up to you to figure out creative discrete ways to implement these. Just make sure that your trigger is the exact same when you are programming it and then applying it.

Sexual Psychic Seduction

1) The sensation of touch is the most important aspect of your visualization.

2) Feel it as if it was happening in the present moment see it as if you were looking at through your own eyes.

3) Never tell anyone that you are using Sexual Psychic Seduction techniques on them.

4) Use your powers to develop yourself at the same time.

5) Try to become more and more creative because your creativity will take you beyond this book.

6) Put your ideas down on paper so you won't forget them.

7) Only use these skills for good.

8) You will get the person you want or someone better, so don't give up during your beginner stage.

9) Flow the unlimited power of the universe through you to realize your goals. Sexual Psychic Seduction done right is not draining it is invigorating.

10) Confidence in yourself brings success that brings confidence in yourself.

Sexual Psychic Seduction

Appendix A

Hermetic Principles

1) Mentalism - All external reality is based on ideas or concepts. The world can be reduced to patterns of potential connections among potential concentrations of matter/energy that might or might not come into form depending upon the introduction of consciousness. The basic force in the universe is mental.

2) Correspondence - One can infer the nature of distant realms from local experience. The dynamics of cells are parallel to the dynamics of galaxies.

3) Vibration - Everything is continual motion. Subatomic particles are continually moving in relation to each other in every concentration of energy and mass in the universe. The patterns of vibration occur in all form - hard rock to vaporous gas to the mental thoughts of humans.

4) Polarity - Things that seem to be opposite of each other are in fact two sides of the same coin. Hot and cold are but different aspects of the same temperature gradient All such polarities are only different vibrations of the same continuum and one can be transmuted into the other.

5) Rhythm - Everything manifest itself in a pattern of back and forth, up and down, in and out. The movement in one direction is compensated for by the return back. Overtime the rhythms result in spiraling shapes that characterize much of the universe.

6) Cause and Effect - What we attribute to "chance' is usually an event whose beginning is not known to us. Every effect has a corresponding cause.

7) Gender - Yin and Yang, chaos and control all describe gender characteristic separate from the everyday human meaning of male and female. The plus and minus aspect of the universe manifests itself in all of creation.

     The Hermetic Principle dates back over five thousand years ago. Only in recent times has scientific measurements caught up with and verified their validity.

     These seven principles are simple keys to the mysteries of matter-energy, spirit-mind and consciousness. They can open the gateways through which a profound transformation of conscious life becomes possible.

Appendix B

Quantum Theory

It's not in the scope of this book to fully explain Quantum Theory but a basic understanding is helpful to your SPS work.

One theory is that an object or outcome of a situation can be in many states at once (superposition) and the final outcome (determination) is dependent on the state being measured, observed or quantified in some manner. If the the state goes unmeasured then all possible outcomes exist.

An example given of Quantum Theory is known as 'Scrödinger's cat'. A cat is placed in a box with a vial of cyanide. We know initially that the cat is definitely in one particular state, because we placed it in the box alive. When we close the lid to the box we cannot see or measure the state of the cat, it maybe alive it may not be if it stepped on the cyanide vial. Quantum Theory says that the cat is in a super-position of two states - it is both dead and alive, it satisfies all possibilities.

Superposition occurs only when the known outcome has not been measured or observed. The act of looking at the cat forces it to be in one particular state, and at that very moment the superposition disappears.

For the purposes of SPS work what Quantum Theory provides is an explanation of why the Hermetic principles only operate in the present. Wanting, wishing and desiring things is equivalent to applying a measurement, a future observation. The mere act wanting, wishing and desiring acts like the reverse polarity of a magnet and continues to push your wants and desires further into the future.

By acting as if your desired outcome already exists you are applying the Quantum Theory that indeed it does exist. By "letting go" of your desire you take away the measurement of wanting that is pushing it away into some distance future.

This may seem like a paradox - act if it exists but let go of the desire for it. This paradox seems to be explained by Quantum Theory. Desire is both a future observation and a measurement - I don't have what I desire (measurement of the present); I would like to have it (future fulfillment). Desire forces a situation from being unknown which allows for all possibilities (including the one you really want) to a known measure which is the present (you don't have what you really want).

If you combine the Hermetic Principle of acting as if what you want already exists with Quantum Theory that what you want does exist as long as you don't measure it in some way then you have a working basis for your SPS work.

Remember to use your SPS work in the following manner:

1) See it, feel it, know it as if it exists now.

2) Let go of the desire and want of it.

3) Repeat step number one.

Know what you visualize is real and exists!

Appendix C

Chakras

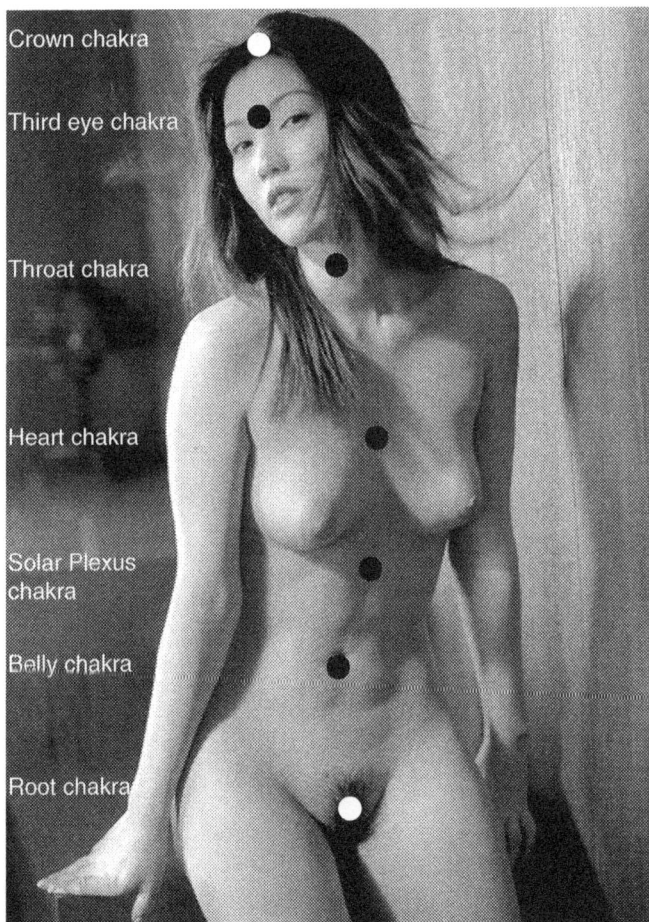

- The Crown chakra is related to the brain, especially the pit-
  uitary and pineal glands.
- The Third Eye chakra is related to vision and the pituitary gland.
- The Throat chakra is related to the lungs and the voice includ
  ing the ears, nose and throat.
- The Heart chakra is related to the heart and circulation.
- The Solar Plexus chakra is related to digestion.
- The Root and Belly chakras is related to generative and
  sexual functions.

The chakras are energy transducers. They serve to integrate physical, emotional, psychological and spiritual facets of the human into a whole being.

Generally speaking the three lower chakras (the root, belly and solar plexus chakras) correlate to basic primary needs - those of survival, procreation and will - and have a larger physiological component to their functioning.

The four higher chakras are more related to our psychological makeup: the heart, throat and third eye chakras are more advanced and more mature, defining love, communication and knowledge. The crown chakra is purely spiritual, providing the connection to the universe beyond.

Appendix D

Merkba

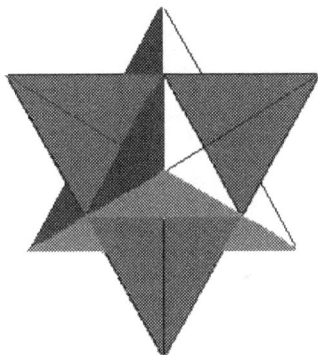

Upward pointing
electrical male tetrahedron.

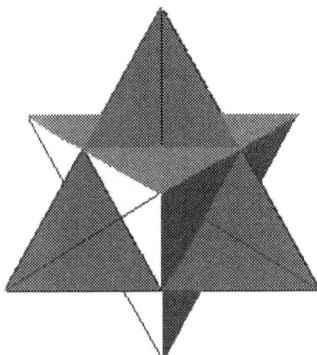

Downward pointing
magnetic female tetrahedron.

Around your body is an energy field that consists of two interlocking tetrahedrons. A tetrahedron is a 3-sided pyramid, which, with the base, makes 4 sides. Each of these 4 surfaces are identical equilateral triangles.

This image on a flat scale is also know as the Star of David (however the true knowledge of this image is still pretty much secret). On a full 3 dimensional scale, this image is a field of energy in the shape of two interlocking tetrahedrons called a Merkaba or Merkabah. You have this field around you however it's probably not activated.

Sexual Psychic Seduction

Appendix E

Sacred Geometry

Everything in the universe follows the same blueprint or patterns created by geometric designs that repeat over and over in an endless combination of light, color and sound.

These universal blueprints are a matrix of grid energy created from a central source which creates the reality in which we experience.

At the physical level of consciousness, souls attach through electromagnetic energy grids which create the illusion of space and time and allow us to experience duality.

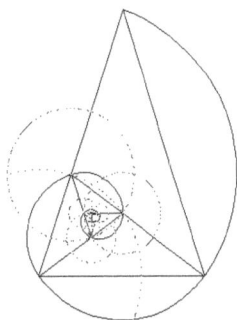

Fibonacci Spiral -

This spiral is the classic shape of the Chambered Nautilus shell. The creature building this shell uses the same proportions for each expanded chamber that is added. Growth follows a law which is everywhere the same.

Flower of Life -

The most important image of sacred geometry is the Flower of Life because within it contains all of creation. Everything is created using this geometric pattern; everything from music, to language, to nature.

Other Best Selling Titles:

How to Become a Porn Director:Making Amateur Adult Films

Dating for the Shy + The Art of Kissing + Threesomes

Asian Dreams

Bare Naked Ladies Series: 4 volume pdf set

Big Chests Small Breasts

Blonde, Beautiful & Bare Naked

Bottoms Up

Desert Delights

Latin Lust

Naked Europe

Sirens

Find these titles at: www.skybluejake.com